Pragmatic Wisdom Vol. 8

Stoic Lessons on Understanding the World

James Bellerjeau

A Fine Idea

Copyright © 2025 by James Bellerjeau

All rights reserved.

No portion of this book may be reproduced in any form without written permission from the publisher or author, except as permitted by U.S. copyright law.

Contents

1. Why Do Anything? An Introduction to the Stoic Lessons — 1
2. On Existence — 3
3. On Fundamental Rules — 9
4. On Studying Beneath the Surface — 16
5. On Studies of Substance — 21
6. On Relative Values — 28
7. On Philosophy's Dividends — 34
8. On Our Rotten Times — 40
9. On What Survives Us — 45
10. On the Independence of Reason — 50
11. On False Fronts — 57
12. On the AI Philosopher — 62
13. On Nature as a Guide — 67
14. On Instincts and Archetypes — 72

Chapter One

Why Do Anything? An Introduction to the Stoic Lessons

Dear friends. Join me on a journey to discover what it means to live a good life. Our inspiration in this quest is Seneca's Moral Letters to Lucilius, revisited and revised for our modern times. The search for what it means to live a good life was not new in Seneca's day, and it will not be old when we are all long gone.

Although these are not Seneca's letters, they honor both his wisdom and his instructions for new students. That is, we should grapple with deep thoughts and make our understanding of the truth personal.

Because no one has a monopoly on the truth, we can each contribute to the puzzle. **The reason to do anything is to answer a question that has not been answered, or at a minimum to answer it for yourself.**

In answering life's deepest questions, would it not be foolish for us to pass by the foundational stones laid by the great thinkers who labored before us? Seneca himself in search of inspiration says in his Letter 2:

> I am wont to cross over even into the enemy's camp, — not as a deserter, but as a scout.

Let us all be avid scouts of the great thinkers, seeking out their every camp with the mindset of anthropologists unearthing meaning from among the ruins. Although Seneca's words have been mined by many for centuries, each generation keeps turning up gemstones.

Thus, with this series of Pragmatic Wisdom for Busy People, let us polish old stones to show them in a new light, and in washing off the mud and debris, reveal what fresh reflections may appear.

Be well.

PS — You can read each of the volumes independently, as it suits your time and your interests. Dedicated readers will find, however, that their understanding of each volume will increase upon reading further volumes. The sincere student may therefore wish to have the full set of Stoic letters: Pragmatic Wisdom for the Sincere Student.

Chapter Two

On Existence

If wishes could create reality, would we live in paradise or hell? I fear we are on the path to finding out

How rich our language is, and how wonderful that it is constantly evolving! We inherit everything bequeathed to us by our ancestors and can dissipate none of the fortune.

Rather, each generation can only add to the riches of the English language. The Oxford English Dictionary defines over 630,000 lexical items as of the year 2020, with more than 860,000 separate senses, or meanings of words.

Words are added to the OED quarterly, at a rate of several thousand per year.

In recent years, the OED has been expanded to include new fears such as *astraphobia* (from ancient Greek, a fear of lightning or thunderstorms accompanied by lightning), *transphobe* (a person prejudiced against transgender people), and *fat-shaming* (the mocking, humiliating, or stigmatizing a person deemed to be fat or overweight).

Though from what the pandemic has already taught us, we have more to fear from COVID-19 than from being told the truth about our weight.

But because the last thing most people want to hear is the truth, we have invented new responses for our new fears including:

- *cancel culture* (publicly boycotting a person thought to be promoting culturally unacceptable ideas) and

- *virtue signaling* (acting in a way motivated primarily by a wish to garner recognition and approval).

- The *keyboard warrior* (one who posts abusive messages on the Internet, typically with a username that conceals his or her identity) is today alone mightier than armies,

- no mere *griefer* (a person who derives enjoyment from spoiling the game for others by playing in a way that is intentionally disruptive and aggravating) but able to breach the stoutest defenses,

- for all we are tempted to dismiss them as a *crybully* (a person who harasses or abuses others yet, following resistance or disagreement, claims to be a victim of ill-treatment).

All around us, some see signs of *structural racism* (discrimination or unequal treatment arising from systems, structures, or expectations that have become established within society), so please *take a knee* (to go down on one knee as a peaceful means of protesting against institutional racism) to start redressing your *unconscious bias* (favoritism towards or prejudice against people of a particular race, gender, or group that influence's one's actions or perceptions) and working off your *white guilt* (remorse or shame felt by a white person with respect to racial inequality and injustice).

I enjoy playing with words, dear reader, and I doubt you will see me tire of it.

Neither do I expect any surcease in the assault on our reason, of which these new words are but the vanguard. Those uttering these inanities are not playing with us, either.

Rather than acknowledging objective truths and adapting themselves accordingly, they wish to redefine reality to suit their subjective wishes.

If wishes could create reality, would we live in paradise or hell? I fear we are on the path to finding out.

In the face of these assaults on my senses, I sought refuge by reminding myself what humankind has learned of existence.

The physics of classical mechanics that busied scientists for the last several thousand years was based on things that humans could observe and directly relate to, including space, time, matter, and energy, and our scales were above the size of the atomic and our speeds below the speed of light.

The high-energy physics of elementary particles departs from this familiar ground and, for many, starts to depart as well from common sense. In quantum mechanics, nature is no longer continuous but rather phenomena are discrete at the atomic and subatomic levels, with waves and particles existing simultaneously in probabilistic states.

Although there have been many attempts to popularize and explain the state of physics today, perhaps the last, best attempt that a layperson could hope to understand was that undertaken by Richard Feynman in the early 1960s in lectures given to undergraduate students at the California Institute of Technology.

Since then, physicists appear only to have added detail and complexity at the cost of clarity and understanding.

Sixty years on, and we are no closer to a grand model unifying relativity and quantum mechanics. Feynman was surely warning us when he said in his very first lecture:

> Everything we know is only some kind of approximation, *because we know that we do not know all the laws yet*. Therefore, things must be learned only to be unlearned again or, more likely, to be corrected.

Though the Standard Model is by far our current best theory, having stood the rigors of many tests, we know it is incomplete.

Indeed, some humility is in order when we admit we do not know what almost all of the universe is made of (dark matter and dark energy indeed), or how to explain the difference in the imbalance between matter and anti-matter.

What we do know is this: unlike its Greek name, the atom can be cut into sub-atomic particles, which are divided into even smaller constituents known as fundamental particles. The Standard Model describes the known fundamental particles and the forces they interact with.

Here is what we think they are.

The twelve known elementary particles of matter or fermions consist of six quarks, designated as up, down, top, bottom, charm, and strange; and six leptons, which can be electrons, muons, and taus, or their neutrino equivalents.

The Standard Model describes how these particles interact via elementary forces called bosons, generating so-called strong, weak, and electromagnetic interactions.

At present, a great unsolved problem is that we cannot account for the force of gravity, and the graviton boson is but hypothetical. The particles of matter exchange gauge bosons, which count among their number gluons, photons, and either Z or W bosons.

The famed Higgs boson, whose existence was predicted decades ago by Peter Higgs, stands alone as a scalar boson.

- After a fifty-year wait the European laboratory for particle physics, CERN, announced in 2012 its detection of the Higgs boson.
- At least the Nobel Prize committee was quicker in granting him recognition for his contribution to our understanding of the nature of existence.

"All well and good," you say, "but what does any of this have to do with living a good life or the meaning of life?"

Not a thing, I suppose, at least not directly. But indirectly, let me suggest the following.

Just as we happily subject ourselves to the stress of vacation travel, on the theory that a change is as good as a rest, so it is with thinking deeply on philosophy. When you need a rest from the strictures of our teaching, take a rest, but make it a change rather than total relaxation.

I have learned the power of continuous improvement can be applied in all areas of life. Small steps taken regularly will let you travel great distances over time, and so it is with your reading.

Steer clear not only of the self-help aisle of the bookshop, dear reader, but you may safely detour around the whole of the "summer reading" section. Though the sun is shining and you are sitting comfortably on the beach, still you may be studying up on some topic that has caught your interest.

If mathematics or physics are not on your Kindle reading list, then still you may enrich yourself with other meaty fare: the development of social and political systems in the Enlightenment, or art and architecture through the ages, to name but a few.

Truly the menu is well stocked despite all you have cut from the dessert section! Besides slowly but steadily adding to your wisdom, when you are thus challenged in your leisure, all the more willingly do you return to the embrace of philosophy when your pause has refreshed you.

We must be deliberate in our actions, whether we are in motion or at rest because this helps us to be consequent in our thoughts.

We humans are no elementary particles, and though our existence is probabilistically uncertain, it is certainly limited. To live long, you must first recognize that you are only living as long as you are living well.

Be well.

Chapter Three

On Fundamental Rules

Any person alive today may yield up answers to the questions that have propelled humankind's search for meaning and for reason

Did I leave you from my last letter with the impression that I am both master builder and in control of my emotions at all times?

You may assume I am prone to exaggeration, dear reader, not so different from the mass media you hear me lament, though my reasons are less vile. Unlike the news, I am not trying to drum up your anger so much as elicit your pity.

Pity me, though, not for failing to live up to my ideals at all times, but for feeling the need to hide that I am flawed. If I should not pretend to be perfect, I would not be so ashamed to miss the mark, thus failing doubly in my thinking.

To atone for my weakness, I will revisit another branch of thinking I have discussed with you before, fundamental physics.

The ancients were the masters of the human condition, and we have yet to match or exceed their analyses of virtue and values, emotion and reason, motivation and action.

But to modern eyes, their understanding of physics missed the mark. Or put differently, we have moved on from their thinking to develop fresh understandings of the workings of our universe.

To use my recent analogy, if the ancients found themselves building a guard's hut by the front gate, successive generations have expanded it to a fortified watchtower, only to abandon these defensive positions altogether for a handsome, full building on the grounds of the estate.

Whether today's knowledge is but a well-appointed guest house, or we have moved into a wing of the grand house itself, we do not know.

For all our progress, dear reader, I think humility is in order.

Despite all that we think we've figured out, we cannot answer fundamental questions about this structure we inhabit. Though to be fair to Seneca, when he asked Lucilius to be the judge of disputed questions, he asked him only to

> state who seems to you to say what is truest, and not who says what is absolutely true. For to do that is as far beyond our ken as truth itself.

Let's review how we've come to know what we presently think is truest, though it may not be the truth yet.

Just as our knowledge of the human condition has been built by accretion through the workings of generations of philosophers adding to the existing corpus, so has the advancement of science proceeded.

How wonderful that any can contribute! The physicist Richard Feynman described the supreme democracy of science in the first of his undergraduate lectures in physics at Caltech:

> We are not concerned with where a new idea comes from — the sole test of its validity is experiment.

What fundamental rules have we learned, first from intuition and hypothesis, and subsequently proven by experiment?

One of the most interesting things we've learned is that we cannot know at the same time both the definite location and the definite momentum of a particle.

This is called the Heisenberg uncertainty principle, and I find it fitting to start with a statement of fundamental uncertainty:

> an inherent property of the quantum systems that make up our reality is that not everything can be determined with precision. For certain fundamental things, we must satisfy ourselves with probabilities.

We think it quite probable the following is a fundamental law: That mass-energy is conserved, which is to say although that mass can be transformed into energy and energy into mass, the quantity of both does not change; and energy [E] and mass [m] are related to one another via the speed of light [c] as captured in the famous formula $E = mc^2$.

Besides this mass-energy equivalence formula, Einstein also gave us

- special relativity (the laws of physics do not change if there is no acceleration between observers; and the speed of light is the same for all observers) and

- general relativity, improving upon Newton's laws of motion themselves to describe gravity as a geometric property of space and time, the curvature of which is related to the energy and momentum of matter and radiation.

Quantum mechanics has undertaken the description of properties of nature at the atomic and subatomic scale. It is from quantum mechanics that we are forced to accept uncertainty as a definite element of nature.

Objects have characteristics of both waves and particles and can be either or both depending on when and how we observe them. From probability amplitudes, we calculate probability density functions to predict where, for example, an electron will be found in an experiment.

Quantum mechanics describes the first three of what we believe are the four fundamental forces or interactions, namely the weak nuclear, strong nuclear, electromagnetic, and gravitation.

ON FUNDAMENTAL RULES

For gravitation, we still rely on Einstein's general relativity. Physicists would dearly love to extend quantum mechanics to explain gravitation and so create a "theory of everything," but quantum gravity has eluded our best efforts.

The physicist who finds a way to not just hypothesize but actually detect the as-yet hypothetical graviton particle will have performed weighty work indeed.

String theorists have proposed frameworks that are intellectually appealing because they give rise to the graviton, but they come at the cost of introducing additional dimensions to the four we currently know, for example, M-theory with its eleven-dimensional model.

The theories have so far yielded insights but no testable hypotheses. Can string theory be considered science at all, then, at least in the way that Feynman describes? Do we need better methods of experimentation, or have we reached the limits of science to explain nature?

I recall from my earlier letter on such topics what reaction I should hear from you now:

"Why are you spending your time on these questions? If they cannot be answered by today's methods, or perhaps ever, what point is there is pondering them? Surely your hours are put to better use in taming your passions and following the lessons that we know are valid."

If one purpose of the study of philosophy is a well-ordered mind, dear reader, then I accept no limits on the ability of my mind to take the lessons of other disciplines.

Indeed, to know that, though countless problems have been solved, countless still remain should give humankind purpose:

we can make progress, we have made progress, and there is progress to be made.

Did nothing exist before a random fluctuation in quantum gravity created the universe from an infinitely hot and dense Big Bang singularity (the so-called no boundary proposal), or was there some First Cause in the form of God that set everything in motion as the Stoics believed?

We think everything we can observe and test today can be explained back to the first 10^{-11} seconds from the creation of the universe.

We speculate on what must have happened in the vanishingly small amount of time *before* this back to zero.

Though we change our scale from the incredibly vast and long to the microscopically tiny and short, the significance of the questions increases.

Any person alive today may yield up answers to the questions that have propelled humankind's search for meaning and for reason.

Although Heisenberg tells us in some realms we must be satisfied with uncertainty, I am sure that humans will never stop searching for meaning.

Is the scientific pursuit so different than our philosophical one? For centuries they were united.

Even though we cannot account yet for every fraction of every second for all time, I say training yourself in fundamental rules from whatever branches of human endeavor you find them is time well spent.

Be well.

Chapter Four

On Studying Beneath the Surface

Why is it so hard to understand what we want, what will make us happy, and how to take the actions that will bring us there?

I have been eagerly anticipating news of your trip to Iceland so that I can hear what you have learned about that island's unique geography.

I am particularly interested to know how your trip to Fagradalsfjall on the Reykjanes peninsula has progressed, and what you've been able to discover about the volcanic eruption ongoing there. This slow-moving and relatively quiet eruption is kind to the observer, allowing an unusually close approach.

How different from the eruptions a decade ago of Eyjafjallajökull, which shot an ash cloud directly into the jet stream resulting in the closure of the entire European airspace and the greatest disruption to air travel in generations.

ON STUDYING BENEATH THE SURFACE

Did you know that we know less about what the core of our own planet consists of than we do the composition of distant galaxies? We train our eyes on the heavens so that we may learn the mysteries of the universe, all the while standing on a mystery only incompletely grasped.

We hypothesize a mostly solid inner core made of an iron-nickel alloy, though we believe there must be other elements in unknown quantities. The inner core is no cold stone but burns with a temperature the same as the surface of the sun.

A liquid outer core surrounds this fiery inner ball, hiding it partly from our probing. Cooling iron at the edge of the core flows in convection currents in the outer core, creating the magnetic field. A great mantle then ensues, topped by a thin crust on which we carry out our lives.

Volcanic activity can be caused by two tectonic plates diverging from one another, allowing hot mantle rock to ooze up under the thinned crust stretched behind the plates; or by two plates colliding, with an oceanic plate typically being pushed under a continental plate, creating magma at the wedge.

Some geologists think that plumes sometimes rise from the core-mantle boundary, melting as they rise and creating volcanoes when plates drift across the plume. For all their fiery drama, most volcanoes happen out of human sight deep under the oceans. Because tiny Iceland perches over a rift in continental plates it has a wealth of volcanoes on display for curious eyes.

The study of philosophy for me is analogous to the study of the geology of the earth. The great volume of what makes us and drives us is hidden, and we spend our lives on the crust.

The surface matter of our lives that all can see is but the tail end of hot, deep processes playing out unbidden and mysterious. Even when we probe within, our senses do not penetrate far and we are left to hypothesize about causes, motivation, and meaning.

Psychologists posit fundamental archetypes found in our collective unconscious, unknown but powerfully shared by all, like the intense hot core at the center of the earth. And just like our knowledge of the earth is meager compared to what we know of the universe, what we understand of our motivations is a fraction of what we can observe of the consequences of our actions.

"What use is this meandering," you ask, "and why should we bother with it?" I will tell you, dear reader, and let me go with the flow of my analogy a bit longer for this purpose.

Just as we find it fascinating to study the flow of magma and explosive volcanic eruptions because they seem to reflect fundamental forces and are elementarily dangerous, so is the study of human motivation and actions of vital interest.

Why is it so hard to understand what we want, what will make us happy, and how to take the actions that will bring us there?

We continue a long tradition of explorers when we take up these questions. It is an honorable inquiry and pursuit. You need not fear that everything valuable about human behavior has been learned, or that the lessons are permanent.

Just like a cloud of volcanic ash can cover the landscape for thousands of miles hiding everything under a choking gray, the passage of time causes people to forget what their forebears have discovered and obfuscates basic truths.

ON STUDYING BENEATH THE SURFACE

We geologists/archaeologists of the mind are sifting the remains of great thinkers, each discovery giving us a chance to both relearn what was once known and to make our own contribution to the sum total of human wisdom.

We too are likely to suffer the fate of all people, which is not only to die but to be forgotten. The great majority are not widely known during their lifetimes, and what of it?

Is it not preferable to be anonymous during your lifetime though you do weighty things, than it is to have achieved temporary renown that fades almost as quickly as our tired and frail bodies? The former has lost nothing, while the latter supposedly progressed only to have the greater setback befall them.

I say our gaze is best directed to *future generations*, dear reader, and it is to them that we shall speak.

The ones who have gone before us are beyond aid. Those who currently share the roads with us are almost as hard to reach because they have a thousand distractions for every core of truth we unearth to shed light on.

Though our contemporaries are most welcome to sample what we have on offer, they have few reliable tools to separate the dishonest potions from the cure. The surest tool is time.

Just like the once choking volcanic ash later turns into a blessing upon nothing more than the passage of time, enriching the soil it blankets with vital nutrients, so too time's great sweep performs the function of separating the silly from the serious, the helpful from the hurtful.

Our good ideas will do the greatest good when they have stood the test of time and proven their worth after careful, considered reflection. We ourselves sift the wisdom of the ancients, which now stands out like volcanic basalt exposed after centuries of erosion have washed all else away.

For us to stand the test of time and have the greatest impact, we must thus spend our time within, applying the lessons of the ancients to our thinking, creating the conditions for well-ordered minds.

Thus honed, reason becomes the tool for humankind to faithfully identify and avoid folly and rather set its sights on building lives of substance.

Be well.

Chapter Five

On Studies of Substance

Rather than wishing you luck and fine things I will wish that you experience hardship, or at least a certain burden

I am not worried about your progress, dear reader, nor your fate. You may suffer bad fortune, illness, or injury because none of us is free from such risks while we are living, but I am confident you will not suffer harm from yourself.

Continue on as you have begun, with an eye towards living modestly and mindfully, and you will live well.

Rather than wishing you luck and fine things I will wish that you experience hardship, or at least a certain burden. This is through no ill will on my part. We become weak and soft in our pampered luxury, whereas privation teaches us to appreciate both what we already have and what is essential.

Your certain burden can come in many forms: It may take the shape of paid work, it may find expression in volunteering; your efforts may be spent on public works, or you may invest in private pursuits.

The end that many seek is an end to their toil, to put their burden down, and this can indeed be a worthy pursuit *provided* it opens the door to other pursuits.

Though you may fight your way free of all external entanglements and purchase your freedom, do not think that idleness is any kind of lasting reward in itself. Indeed, the longer you seek to enjoy idleness, the less you stand to gain from it.

The freer your hands are from manual labor, the more your mind is at risk from laboring under apprehensions and worries. You can be far removed from the dank salt mines where others toil but still feel as sharply the lash of your own expectations and fears.

Thus, I tell you do not put down all burdens when your time is more completely yours to direct. Turn once more to your studies to ensure that you do not lose your way and continue to progress.

Is it the study of philosophy that is required? Helpful, always helpful, but I would not say required, at least in the case of one like yourself whose lessons have been well learned and are never far from memory. By all means, refresh your recollection, and take pleasure in strolling even the best-known and well-loved by-ways of your favorite teachers.

But if you find your tastes turning to other things, let your mind roam freely and wander.

In your wandering, you will likely find that you do not know every path as well as you remembered. Though you stray in your contemplations, you will thus remain on the path to wisdom.

For this to happen you cannot be a passive tourist, watching new landscapes unfold from a safe distance and behind glass. Rather take your current learnings and see how they may be actively applied in new settings: Psychology, politics, physics, and more.

Will you make a connection between two fields that no one has managed to bridge before? Will you develop a wholly new line of thinking? Even if you provide merely a fresh perspective in an area previously believed to be fully understood, you will have acted nobly and invested the energy of your thoughts well.

And I ask you, at this moment is there any field as falsely believed to have been mapped as that of human motivation? We think we are entitled to talk about what drives others when we have the slightest idea of what drives ourselves.

Maslow's hierarchy of needs can be set out in a neat pyramid, with basic needs anchoring the bottom, psychological needs forming the middle, and self-fulfillment needs at the tip. Until the basic needs of food and water, safety, and shelter are satisfied, the theory goes, a person cannot work their way upwards to achieve a higher purpose.

In fairness, this is little different than what the Stoics and many other philosophical schools busied themselves with: What is the relative value of various human pursuits, and which should we pursue and why.

There have been as many interpretations of human motivation as there have been people who have pondered their own existence. Hundreds of serious schools of thought, some easily dismissed in hindsight, but others with enduring elements of the truth.

I do not doubt that generations to come will offer up additional valuable insights. No, we need not fear that the study of human motivation will be wasted time, for no matter whether you establish a new branch of wisdom, you will surely help yourself.

Or take the study of human intelligence and how inconsistently and even apprehensively modern theorists approach it.

Before they realized how their measurements would be misinterpreted and misused, psychologists developed quite reliable methods of measuring general human intelligence, or IQ (intelligence quotient). We are able to measure it more accurately than any other psychometric measure.

Not only can we measure it well, but psychologists have found that intelligence is the single most important determinant of life success. At least it is predictive in terms of educational and economic success, which we know is not everything, but it is also not nothing.

Psychologists also believe that intelligence is largely genetic and that although it can be influenced by environmental factors, the influence comes mainly in ways that either allow genes to express themselves or hinder the full development of potential intelligence.

Despite the weight of significant evidence, it is considered a cardinal sin in today's world to state that intelligence drives important life outcomes while also pointing out that people's individual intelligence differs.

Why is this so? We accept that people have physical differences that are apparent to the eye: the muscular athlete, the handsome actor, the model with symmetric features. Perhaps these differences are easier for us to swallow because we can tell ourselves that it is the steroids and supplements or the plastic surgeon's knife that have contributed to their enhanced natures.

Physical differences it seems are much easier to accept than the idea that our fates have been determined by a genetics lottery at birth, and that these gifts of fate are distributed unevenly.

Though we can no longer say it aloud, we can nonetheless silently observe that people also differ in their intelligence and temperament. To see something so important and yet restrict discussion because of the possibility of offending! Truly people can be willfully ignorant no matter what their intelligence.

I had despaired of advances in this field, dear reader, but I think there is a parallel path down which we might once again see progress. It concerns what is called artificial general intelligence, or AGI.

If the study of human differences is taboo let us heat up our brains in trying to make cold circuits and wires think. In trying to create intelligence in computer form, we may yet learn something about how humans think, though this is not the aim of the endeavor.

So become an indirect scientist, divining insights about human capabilities and motivation from our successes and, more likely, the failures of artificial intelligence research.

The most attractive aspect of working in this field is that we are perpetually on the cusp of breakthroughs. It is a magical feat that no matter how many decades we labor we are never further than a decade away from achieving AGI.

The last seventy years have at least humbled us to the point where we appreciate the magnitude of the problem. The human brain is no simple box of cells that we can replicate at will. By narrowing our ambition and our scope, we have unblocked a half-century's stall and seen rapid progress in artificial neural networks, pattern recognition, and machine learning.

And even if you want to leave the hard science to others, there is still a role to play for the philosopher with time on their hands. We have spent centuries experimenting to discover which models of societal governance best balance human weaknesses with human potential to let the most citizens thrive.

In AGI research the large majority of scientists are interested foremost in the question of *how*, as in how can we do it? A few have considered the question of *why*, and fewer still the question of *whether* we should do this.

We need but recall the mad dash to split the atom, with everything that was subsequently unleashed, to know that the smartest among us can also be the most reckless.

The long-term survival of humanity needs much more attention invested in the question of *control* of AGI.

Religions all assume an omnipotent creator, who is all-knowing and all-seeing, and has the power to direct all affairs. Consider though that if humankind had a creator, could it not be that our author was both unimaginably more powerful than us but similarly reckless? That in unleashing humankind on the world, they lost control and no longer have any say in determining our fate?

I do not mean to make humans think of themselves as gods if and when we bring AGI into being. My aim is more that we consider what sort of creators we would be if we had no means of directing the course of our new creation.

Chances are good that we will not have the luxury of centuries to experiment with how to control AGI. This genie being unloosed will not go willingly back into any bottle.

Thus, this would be a study worthy of serious pursuit by serious minds. Perhaps it will be you?

Be well.

Chapter Six

On Relative Values

I can't help but think how much the Stoics would have benefitted from exploring the beauty of set theory

No, dear reader, do not envy me for bidding farewell to my alarm clock. I can give you at least four reasons why not.

In the first place, envy is a known disturbance of the mind, an encroachment on your otherwise well-ordered reason. What another has is wholly irrelevant to what *you* have, just as your possessions, both material and immaterial, are irrelevant to the happiness of others.

It is the obsessive focus on the differences between people that arouses their passions. Once aroused, few of these passions are then put to the betterment of humankind.

We can level the field far more easily by tearing down those who excel than by raising up the many who cluster at the center of the bell curve, to say nothing of the long tail to the left.

If only we could bring ourselves instead to note all the ways in which we have already far exceeded others, and upon so noticing bend down a helping hand to pull them up. But instead, despite the hordes we have passed, we cast our envying gaze at the ones who remain ahead of us.

The additional reasons why you need not envy me can be enumerated as follows.

- My bladder and my prostate have conspired to create a more effective biological alarm than my digital clock ever mustered. And this all too human siren rouses me not just once a night like my prior electronic minder, but two, three, even four times.

- Then there is the fact that I seem to *need* less sleep than before. Though my labors are extensive, and I slip under my covers with an exhausted sigh, still my body sometimes pops awake before my mind thinks it suitable.

- And my mind itself presents the final reason for your pity and not envy: I *want* less sleep than I need. Though the measure of a life is whether it is well-lived and not whether it is long, I long to experience as much of my remaining life as possible. Thus, I have given up my alarm just when I find I need it least.

Sometimes when I am lying awake, I will nonetheless remain in my bed, for my body also knows when it is too early to rise even though my mind is already at work. A turn of phrase may spontaneously arise from which a train of thought starts chugging along.

These thoughts used to drive me unwillingly from my sheets to my desk to capture them in words, for fear that they would either keep me from sleep or that I would lose them altogether.

My mantra of late has been to simply say, "Let it go. It's OK, let it go."

I seem to have no lack of thoughts or words these days. So, if the thought is worthy, I expect I will be reinspired soon enough. And if not, there has been nothing lost by letting these ephemeral night visitors float away.

Often my wandering thoughts turn to the Stoics, and how far we can follow their teachings before stumbling or, worse, running up against a brick wall. The simplicity and firmness of approach has its own appeal, but there is also danger in dogmatism.

Is there but a single virtue to be found in reason, and must all external things be considered of secondary value? Is it possible for the mind to be master of all circumstances, no matter what comes? And what does that make a person, and is it enough?

Given the importance the Stoics placed on the development of reason, and their use of deductive reasoning and logic, I can appreciate why they sometimes let their thoughts carry them to extremes.

Competing schools sought to tie each other in syllogistic knots, by taking an accepted proposition and extending it further and further until they produced a paradox. These paradoxes were then held out as proof that the whole proposition or value statement was untrue, or at least severely undermined.

On the one hand, the existence of a paradox presents us with a seeming problem. If the logic we have followed is sound, that must mean a defect in one or more of the propositions we began with. At the same time, paradoxes represent opportunities to reflect more deeply on what we think we understand and why, and possibly to advance the frontier of human understanding beyond where it currently lies.

For many serious students though, to say nothing of generations of casual readers, the insistence on following logic from set propositions to their inevitable conclusions sometimes led the Stoics to defend extreme positions that defied common sense:

- A single day lived according to the ultimate good of a reasoned mind was exactly equal to and as valuable as a hundred years in the same condition.

- Dying young upon the torturer's rack after betrayal and unjust accusations was no more to be feared than slipping away peacefully in old age.

It is the state of mind that matters: The wise man fears nothing that is inevitable and according to nature.

Short of seeking to conquer death, or at least the fear of death, the Stoics had much advice about avoiding vice, and all the things external to people that aroused their passions and cost them their self-possession.

The Stoic proposition is that living according to reason is the highest and only virtue. Further, that virtue is sufficient for a happy life. The instant you feel you are lacking something external you have disturbed your reason for something ultimately without value because the only thing of value is your well-ordered mind.

It does not matter what happens to you or what circumstances you find yourself in, it matters how you react to your circumstances. The virtuous person cannot be harmed by being poor, or ill, or any of the things that normally so trouble us.

I can't help but think how much the Stoics would have benefitted from exploring the beauty of set theory. I think they would have taken to it naturally, and found ways to extend even our modern understandings.

At a minimum, a Venn diagram illustrating the logical relationship between sets might have helped them work out from underneath at least a few of the seeming paradoxes that plagued them.

For example, though mathematical logic was put to use by philosophers hundreds of years before the earliest Stoics, it is only since the late 1800s that we have updated our understanding of infinity, using set theory to prove that although there is an infinity of infinities, some infinities are larger than others.

Set theory has had its own paradoxes to contend with, but our field of correct application is very broad though we limit ourselves to the von Neumann universe of pure sets.

Or take Bayesian probability, which introduces reasonable expectation to the concept of probability, instead of mere likelihood and frequency. The student of Bayesian statistics updates probabilities upon obtaining new data, computing conditional probability and distributions of probability.

Better answers are arrived at by taking prior knowledge but also personal beliefs into account. From a philosophical perspective, should we not welcome making room for human emotions and not requiring people to act like mere reasoning machines?

Armed with such theories and logical weapons, would modern Stoics find that no emotion or disturbance to reason could be tolerated? Would their belief in cardinal virtues and how they best expressed themselves have been shaken or extended by allowing relativity into their calculations?

I do not know the answer to these questions, dear reader, though these thoughts are much on my mind. Will you help me by sharing your perspective?

Wisdom is neither the possession of one people or one time nor a fixed thing. It is the individual pursuit by each of us who takes up the task of casting what light we can, building upon all who have gone before us.

Be well.

Chapter Seven

On Philosophy's Dividends

Philosophy's domain is in guiding decisions about what we do with what we have, and how we respond to the circumstances we face

If there was a time when people lived in abundance and without any cares, perhaps it was when the first humans cavorted in the Garden of Eden.

From the time we ate of the Tree of Knowledge people have possessed reason. Since then, we were cast out of our period of easy plenty and have had to make our way in the world in lives of toil and struggle.

This has given many cause to ask the question "Is there any way for us to regain our carefree lives of abundance?"

The question I want to address today is whether and to what extent philosophy has contributed to the betterment of humankind in our wanderings through hard times.

If we have seen our lot improve over time, how much of it has come from philosophy and how much from other sources, including humankind itself through the application of science?

You could argue that intelligence is humankind's greatest gift, for all that it led to our losing paradise. Like all great things, intelligence is not one-dimensional. Its application can also be our greatest curse.

We have conquered the planet and have dominion over everything on it. But we have not conquered our desires. Further, by virtue of our nature to seek dominance over all things, we cannot avoid seeing hierarchy in everything.

Thus, having overcome the natural world our eyes turn to our fellow citizens. The result is that we are subject to a wealth of harmful emotions, such as greed, fear, jealousy, and anger.

Having "more," as in more wealth, beauty, possessions, or power, affords us greater stature in the hierarchy. This inclines us to always seek more. But no matter how much we have, we cannot make ourselves happy.

This is because in every hierarchy there are better off and worse off. Thus, everyone who sees someone above them is inclined to feel worse off than they otherwise might if they understood that peace of mind is the greatest possession of all.

In consequence, rather than being closer to regaining our carefree lives, the more abundance we acquire the farther we find ourselves from happiness and satisfaction. The pursuit of *more* thoroughly blinds most of us to seeing and understanding that to live a happy life one only needs that which is *enough*.

The aim of philosophy is to ensure we make proper use of our greatest gift, which is reasoning intelligently.

Humans alone are not forced to live as mere animals, subject to ungoverned emotions and physical urges. We can use reason not with the purpose of reigning in and extinguishing our ambitions, but to give them purposeful direction.

We should accept what we are given by nature and work to improve upon it. We should strive to theorize, invent, and explain but let it be in directions of our choosing after measured reason. If we seek to excel, to create, and to explore, let us do it knowingly, not blindly, and certainly not just because we can.

Do you honor someone who says they climbed a mountain just because it is there? That is as much of a reason as Cain saying he killed Abel because he was there. "I could, so I did" is not reasoned thinking.

Of course, there is a motive behind the climber and the killer, though they may not be able to articulate it aloud. Is it the place of philosophy to curb these impulses, to tame all humankind's passions? Just as intelligence is both a blessing and a curse, let us not consign reckless ambition to being entirely useless.

Who else but the ambitious would undertake dangerous missions that occasionally advance the human race by great leaps and bounds? Who else but the reckless would leap to the defense of their fellow persons at great cost to their own safety?

We should revel in our prowess as material creatures, not because physical prowess is virtuous in and of itself, but because it is part of our nature that allows us to overcome all obstacles.

So, intelligence and ambition are both fundamental parts of human nature. Philosophy can take no credit for our natures and everything that springs from them.

ON PHILOSOPHY'S DIVIDENDS

Philosophy's domain is in guiding decisions about what we do with what we have, and how we respond to the circumstances we face. It takes work to become wise because we need to learn to trust neither the surface appearance of things nor the opinions of the majority on most things.

All the greatest human accomplishments were achieved by intelligent people but not necessarily wise people.

The participants in the Manhattan Project understood in theory how to split the atom and they found a way to put their theories into practice. How often does humankind need to repeat the lesson that knowledge once gained is scarcely to be contained?

So, we suffered yet another fall from grace, again at our own hands. The fruit of that discovery has meant humankind living in fear not just of being yet further from a carefree life, but of life's very existence being extinguished from the earth.

I have written separately about the unchecked enthusiasm among artificial intelligence researchers. I see in them the similar bravado of the mountain climber facing a peak not yet summited. We will do it because it can be done!

Do you doubt for a moment that the joy researchers feel upon the first human-created intelligence emerging will be outdone many times over with bitter remorse at what we once again unleashed unwittingly on ourselves and the world?

Philosophy's dividends are this, dear reader: To first identify the right questions for humankind to be asking, and then to apply the very same reasoning the scientist uses in answering them.

- These questions include "What is of true value and how can we go about achieving it?"

- Not the question of what are all the things we *can* do, but "*Why* should we do what we do?"

- We do not question whether we can live in a world that is both easy and fair. It is clear we cannot remake the world fully to our liking. Rather we ask and answer the question "How can I conduct myself in every circumstance including, and even especially, hard and unfair circumstances?"

We do not lack clever scientists in the world. Intelligence has been fruitful and multiplied along with humanity and our ambition knows no bounds.

The world is overflowing with theories, inventions, and ideas. How many of them have made life better? I don't mean convenient, easier, or more productive. How many of our modern wonders have made us *happier*?

No, I tell you we do not need more intelligent scientists, we need more wise scientists. We need the philosopher-scientist to stop and think before acting.

"But" the scientific community will say, "if we do not pursue this line of inquiry, someone else will." They will continue, "You cannot hold back progress by refusing to study and to learn."

It is not all progress that we should be seeking to forestall, but progress in harmful directions.

We know there is pain and danger and risk in the world. Must we truly open every door that is closed and walk down every path that is shaded to relearn again and again that not every development is beneficial?

Philosophy would teach us that the ultimate power we can wield is not over nature but over ourselves.

Do you know what we will find when we set aside our lust for power, our greed for possessions, and our endless jealousy? The realization that we never left the Garden of Eden and that we can return to it at any time if we simply open our eyes to see it.

Be well.

Chapter Eight

On Our Rotten Times

Just as advances and accomplishments belong to an age in history, so too do the embarrassments that the next generation takes but a few decades to clearly perceive

Have you noticed that each generation inevitably becomes convinced of two things, dear reader?

- First, they have reached the pinnacle of wisdom with current science and civilization; that their way of life and pursuits are correct and good and the one true path.

- And second, they simultaneously laugh at how their ancestors were so gullible and dangerously ignorant in so many things; while they lament that their children are both gullible and dangerously ignorant in so many things.

ON OUR ROTTEN TIMES

"Contemptible idiots behind us, and superficial fools ahead of us! Howsoever will the world survive when we are gone?"

It is not the times that give rise to such convictions. The folly is peculiar to humankind itself and so passes unbidden and unseen from generation to generation.

It is true that each generation finds a way to express its failings uniquely. Just as advances and accomplishments belong to an age in history, so too do the embarrassments that the next generation takes but a few decades to clearly perceive.

Humans are powerful in so many things but applying perspective to our *own* imperfections is not one of our inherent talents, nor do we seem to have any desire to develop it.

Is our own generation really the first to be free from error? Have we become enlightened as a whole, such that our every utterance deserves to be inscribed in the skies for all to wonder at?

Let us seek to be impartial judges and consider the evidence.

- We live in times where serious people seriously expound the idea that you can tell something important about the inside of a person by looking only at the outside of that person.

- That all of society can be explained by power, and that there is no objective reality behind power structures, only self-serving and self-perpetuating identity groups.

Consider the supposed attributes of "whiteness," which we are told have been invented and used to oppress non-white people.

- These include that whites value self-reliance, rational linear thinking, and the idea that hard work is the key to success.

- That it makes sense to plan for the future, delay gratification, and make progress.
- That we should have an action orientation and seek to master our circumstances.

Before you find yourself nodding along in agreement with the items on the list, recall that they are held out as symbols of oppression, not freedom.

Social justice movements hold out as heroes the victims of police brutality, as if somehow resisting arrest is the better example of virtuous conduct. Among the most exalted are the ones who have been martyred, and it does not seem to matter what their prior record may have been.

Mobs vandalize and burn city streets and we call it justice. Crowds loot stores and we call it redistribution of wealth. City councils tell you they expect to see *less* crime when they defund the police and stop prosecuting offenders.

For our own parts, we fill our bellies with junk food and we fill our heads with junk science. We buy junk products on credit and amuse ourselves with junk entertainment to tickle our ever-shortening attention spans.

We go into debt to pay for educations that fill our children's heads with dangerous nonsense. We borrow money to buy cars and houses that we don't need and can't afford.

All this brings us more sadness than satisfaction in both the pursuit and the possession.

On the national level, our politicians have elevated empty talk to a new art form. With one side of their mouths, they stoke our most base emotions and outrage.

So aroused, with our eyes burning red and our ears ringing, we do not notice when they utter out of the other side things like, "There are no limits on what we can spend and there is no consequence to running our deficit higher and higher."

As if! This is one time when future generations will look back not in amusement but in horror at the delusions we felt comfortable with, for we are burdening them with both our sins of omission as well as those we commit.

No, we would know on a moment's quiet reflection that ours is not the golden age, dear reader. At least, no more than any other age.

Despite our advancements in science, technology, health care, productivity, and more, we have spent little time in the laboratory of the human soul. For all our progress in external things, we have forgotten that the natural course of our minds inclines downward.

Stability in human societies is only ever temporary. We fail and we have never not failed.

The reason is that we have never removed our weaknesses and our vices from the equation. We have too few examples of virtuous behavior, and pay too little attention to the examples we have, for them to tip the scales in our favor.

In their hearts, people are not so easy to fool. We know when we are consuming garbage, though none admits it aloud.

We suffer in our hearts and our thoughts when we proclaim satisfaction with superficial things. These internal maladies do not remain suppressed but are expressed through ill health, depression, and turmoil in society.

Thus, we have sown the conditions for our downfall: Those who are told they are well-off are nonetheless unfulfilled and so restless and eager for change; while those who are told they are suffering are angry and mobilized to tear down the systems that have failed them.

Who will fight to preserve the good that humankind has achieved in its centuries of struggle? Who will ensure that the good humankind is capable of is not extinguished in the fire along with everything else?

In our rotten times, you cannot stand on the sidelines. You are either pouring water on the flames or you are fanning them. By your silence you let the rot spread.

By your words, do you seek to build and fortify or only tear down?

The early few may sacrifice themselves in standing up against madness, true. But if none stand, all will fall. And perhaps we will find that there are others who will stand with us to slow the fall.

Be well.

Chapter Nine

On What Survives Us

Serving as an example is more powerful than lingering in memory. What will people say about your conduct when you're g one?

In an earlier exchange, I gave you the argument for making plans for the future and doing your best to execute your plans.

You have reminded me of what I usually remind you, namely that we can take nothing with us past our own deaths. This leads naturally to the next question you have posed, "Does anything of our works survive after we are gone?"

If you grant me leave to first broaden your question somewhat, dear reader, I will give you my answer. The broader topic I wish to address is whether *anything* survives us, and if so what.

I have said that when we pass on our possessions remain. This was in the context of acknowledging that we cannot take material things with us into the immaterial zone beyond life.

So, it seems that while we do not survive our possessions, they survive us. We know not what will be made of them, though we may will them to others via our testamentary disposition.

Do we know if our wishes will be honored? We do not. You know I will continue on to say it does not matter, at least as far as the deceased is concerned.

Some of our friends and acquaintances can be expected to survive us, and children too if we have brought them into the world. They will each carry memories of us with them for a time.

We act according to reason for the sake of acting properly, and not to burnish our reputation. But if we have acted properly in our lives, it is appropriate for people who knew us well to hold positive memories of us after we have passed on.

Our conduct can also serve as an example to all those we encountered during our lifetimes. Pray let it be an example of good conduct rather than an example of what to avoid!

Serving as an example is more powerful than lingering in memory. The memory serves to remind someone of what *we* once did, whereas your example is an exhortation for what *they* are to do now.

If we are to be remembered, I would rather it was for conduct serving as a good example than mere memories of fine times and glad doings.

"What of our work" you ask, "and the things we have laid down in writing? Surely this is a more permanent record that will survive our demise."

I am not so sure, dear reader. I have seen many people come and go in the work setting. Some are tempted away by greener grass elsewhere, others are lured into early retirement.

Though the colleagues are soon gone their files remain stubbornly behind. Lawyers and accountants in particular trail great masses of paper behind them, like the wake of a supertanker.

The ranks of forests have been thinned if we take as evidence the organized rows of binders you are likely to find in the office of the tax specialist, to say nothing of the voluminous case files chronicling once important disputes shepherded along by lawyers.

These materials may be no more than a decade old. Have a stranger leaf through the volumes and they will be as indecipherable as hieroglyphics were to generations of Egyptologists.

"Well, what of our good deeds" you wonder, "and the things we have set in motion with our planning? Do our plans necessarily come to naught because we ourselves necessarily do?"

This is a more interesting question and again calls to mind some differences between our modern times and those of the ancients. If our ancestors made it seem that everything ended with their own existence it is because it must have seemed so to them.

When generals conquered territories, only to have them retaken a short while later, and Emperors could not rest easy on their thrones for a moment, what hope did the average person have that their works would endure?

We have been experimenting with different forms of society and political community for some time. At least since the Enlightenment we have created some that are more enduring than others.

The rule of law has been introduced and entrenched. It has brought with it the fantastic concept that we are nations ruled not by the whims of people but by written laws. No person is above the law and as a result, the creation of the law cannot be so easily undone by the undoing of a single person.

I refer to legal entities like corporations or foundations.

A legal entity is a real thing, dear reader, at least as real as our hopes, fears, and dreams. They have greater power than the thoughts that course through our minds because they can accomplish tangible things in the world through the human agents that work in their service.

A corporation may survive a succession of CEOs, each carried out the door by mandatory retirement age if not carried off before then by some other corporate intrigue. Though twenty CEOs have come and gone, the corporation is as vital as ever.

You can argue whether people dead for generations should have continued influence on the living, for example through their foundations. But you cannot argue that nothing of their will has survived their deaths.

The Swedish chemist Alfred Nobel died in the 1890s, but before leaving the mortal world he decreed the bulk of his fortune be used for the annual award of the Nobel Prize. It is given in multiple disciplines to persons who "have conferred the greatest benefit to humankind." What a legacy!

I could say the names Rockefeller, Wallenberg, and Duke; or Ford, Nemours, and Lilly, and chances are most people will have heard of at least some of them.

Foundations created by them all, with billions in endowment. They were created by people no person living today ever met, but they live on in their good works.

So yes, the good deeds that we have set in motion with our planning can indeed survive us, and for long after our deaths.

Your aim in setting long-term plans is not to enhance your reputation. Your reputation will be gone not long after you are.

No, you should make your plans to take advantage of the power of time to deliver the greatest good to the greatest number.

This can indeed bring you wide renown and many generations may know your name. Does it matter that *you* will not know it and your beneficiaries will never know you?

Be well.

Chapter Ten

On the Independence of Reason

A wise person's reasoned judgment must come to the same conclusion when presented with the same facts

You asked the question with such seeming innocence, "Does reason exist as an independent thing?"

I wonder if you know how important this question is. That we have arrived at the crux of what we have been discussing, and the implications of the answer are far-reaching.

Well, I need not build up your expectations for a grand answer too quickly. Let me rather start constructing the framework more modestly from the ground up.

To ask whether reason exists independently is to question whether it depends on the person or on the situation.

- In other words, will two people looking at the same situation come to the same well-reasoned conclusions?

- Will one person looking at two situations at different times come to the same conclusions both times?

- Does it matter who applies reason, what is the context, and what are the consequences of a decision?

Another way to ask the question is this. Assume we had before us a person of perfect wisdom, whose ability to apply the reason of their well-ordered mind was reliably demonstrated, Socrates say.

Could Socrates tell us the reasoned answer to every situation, for every person, every time? And assuming we have no trouble believing this to be the case, now ask yourself the question, "Would Aristotle agree in every case with Socrates?"

If two wise persons do not agree every time in every detail, is it the fault of the wise persons, or the fault of the situations they are discussing, or the fault of reason itself?

So, is the wise person not truly wise, in that their thinking has not attained true reason at least in part? Are some situations simply amenable to unvarying answers? Or is reason an entirely independent thing that gives us a consistent answer regardless of who applies it?

Having reflected on these questions, it seems to me at first glance that the teachings of philosophy and law suggest different answers to the question.

The philosophy of human thought has been a story of evolution, with ideas being proposed, debated, and refined by successive generations. If nothing else, our understanding of the physical world has advanced significantly, relegating early scientific theories to quaint historical footnotes.

And our understanding of the workings of the mind is also far advanced, though there remains much we cannot explain. This suggests a progression towards more perfect reason, rather than simply describing its operation.

But philosophers are not shy about suggesting their ideas are not just correct directionally, but also absolutely. You will no doubt recall how many times I have given you instruction by exhortation rather than entreaty.

Did you understand me all this time to be making mere suggestions for your improvement rather than commandments on how to live a good life? No, although they may disagree vehemently with one another, individual philosophers have not been shy about saying that they have found basic truths that apply in all circumstances.

Is this yet another paradox for which philosophy is famous? Not necessarily, dear reader. Although it is certainly possible that two sure-minded philosophers are both wrong, it is equally possible that they are both right.

"Now you are confusing me. How can you resolve a paradox with another paradox?"

I am not trying to be clever here. Consider that when two philosophers appear to disagree, they are often starting from different premises or describing alternative cases.

Much of what frustrates me about philosophical debates is that they devolve into petty disagreements about the meaning of words. Words have meaning, but if your case hinges on the definition of one word and mine depends on another, then it is more likely we are doing little more than talking past each other and missing the underlying truth.

I think this also explains the approach taken by the law. I said earlier that law and philosophy seem to supply different answers.

In philosophers, you will find many who say, "I have found the answer, and it is this." In law, you will hear rather "Reasonable minds can disagree."

People think lawyers are not humble, but in this case, I must concede that the lawyers' approach is the more modest one. But I give no profession a free pass, and for the moment I want you to consider that the statements of both philosophy and law are wrong.

Philosophy is wrong insofar as it suggests there is but one answer.

Take the hard science of math, which is built upon firm logical ground. Math is full of equivalents. These are terms or statements that represent a certain value and may be substituted for one another.

Why should something so complex as human affairs permit only a single, unvarying answer? Could there be many solutions to a problem, all equally correct? It is not so much that my answer is right and your answer is wrong, so much as perhaps both answers are right because they are equivalent.

If the purpose of philosophy is to help people lead good lives, then should not the answers offered up be as varied as the people they are supposed to aid?

As appealing as this line of thought is, dear reader, we should be careful in pursuing it too far. For you are but a single step away from saying that reason is relative. That it depends not only on the situation, but on the person, and thus must be entirely subjective.

If a solution works for a person, then it works. This person finds relief in reading, that person in shopping, another in drinking — they are each happy and who are we to say they are wrong? But this means there is no fundamental reason, just pragmatism applied to wishful thinking.

I say it is a step too far to conclude *all* answers are valid just because there may be more than *one* valid answer.

So, do the lawyers have the better take? When they say "reasonable minds can disagree," they do not mean that *any* interpretation is valid, but that there may be more than one reasonable interpretation. An objective judge or jury can still audit the chain of thought and see which conclusions reasonably follow.

If philosophers are criticized for assuming one answer applies to all situations, lawyers make another mistake: They assume one situation can permit many answers.

The fact that reasonable minds can differ is not because there are multiple interpretations of the same facts, but that the same situation has multiple facts in play.

So Lawyer A strings together a line of facts that support Conjecture A, and Lawyer B pulls a related but different set of facts from the same situational soup and finds the ingredients for Conjecture B. They are both reasonable in constructing their logical arguments. But they are not arguing different conclusions from the same facts, rather different conclusions from different facts.

"I am now thoroughly confused," you say. "You have told me philosophers are wrong for saying that a single solution applies in all cases, and lawyers are wrong in saying reason can be applied differently to the same facts. How does this help answer the question of whether reason exists independently, which I am now rather regretting asking you?"

Do not despair, dear reader. The conclusion of my argument is near at hand, as is the conclusion of today's letter.

What squabbling philosophers and squabbling lawyers have in common when they disagree is that they are arguing different cases (always assuming they are dealing honestly).

Socrates and Aristotle *would* come to the same conclusion if they were presented with the same facts in the same way. The reason is, in my view, that reason is *not subjective*. It only seems so because it is always interpreted by us as individuals.

- This person may have a harder time letting go of possessions because of their upbringing, the habits and vices they inculcate, and the friends they surround themselves with.

- That person may find it all too easy to scorn public opinion because they never found public favor and so placed little value on it.

Just as the situations we each face inevitably differ, we each have a unique history that creates the personal conditions we bring to each situation. Virtue is found in neither the person nor their situation but in their application of reason to their situation.

And this reason, I posit, never changes. A wise person's reasoned judgment must come to the same conclusion when presented with the same facts. When everything appears relative, it is only the observer that changes, and not the fundamental forces that apply to our actions.

Hence, I conclude that reason does exist independently and absolutely. It is our individuality that tricks us into wanting to give reason a sliding scale of application.

Apply your judgment to every situation by listening to reason and not emotion, and you will not be so easily led astray.

Be well.

Chapter Eleven

On False Fronts

We take at face value the whole of our lives. In refusing to think for yourself, you resign yourself to accept the same fate as others

I remember going on an excursion with my family when I was a young boy. This would have been in the late '70s or early '80s, when we would spend six weeks of the hottest and brightest summer months away from the Kingdom of Saudi Arabia where my father worked and our family lived.

We traveled from an oasis in one arid country to a desert in another in the province of Almeria, Andalusia. This part of Spain is mountainous, rugged, filled with cacti and the crumbling remains of once vast industrial works.

The Mediterranean glinted invitingly, its clear blue water stretching out of sight into the horizon as if to mock the very idea that we sat baking in the middle of the driest part of the European continent.

Stay in any place for too long and you will take everything for granted. The iron-red mountains, with their herb-covered foothills running down to the azure sea, became so much painted backdrop to the boredom playing out within the four walls of our house.

So it was that my parents herded my brothers and me into the car one day for a drive to Tabernas, where the tantalizingly named Mini Hollywood nestled. This was where Sergio Leone filmed the spaghetti Western For a Few Dollars More, and where the drama of The Good, the Bad and the Ugly unfolded.

How could this not be a magical place to visit?

As an adult, dear reader, I can tell you the distance to the kilometer, but back then it was a journey into the unknown.

And like any journey when you do not know the destination, but whose arrival you eagerly anticipate, it seemed to take forever. I could not have spent half a day of my life staring out the window onto thousands of square kilometers of scrub and sand, but I felt older by the time we were freed from our four-wheeled prison.

Look! A genuine Western town, starting with the town square, watering trough for horses, and the storefronts facing it on all sides.

- The Yellow Rose Saloon, the Fire Company, Overland Stage Lines.

- A schoolhouse, the General Merchandise Store, and is that a church steeple I see?

A whole town laid out for us to walk through, not as spectators but as participants, transported directly into another world only ever seen on screen.

There was some sort of show, cowboy stunts, perhaps a recreated bank robbery. I don't recall exactly.

The appearance of actors and the carrying out of assigned roles had the effect, for me at least, of making it seem *less* real. No matter how lifelike, the play could not compare to the rich dramas concocted in my mind.

For the same reason, I suppose, that even the best film adaptation of a favorite book inevitably disappoints. "That's not how I imagined it when I was reading it," goes the resigned realization. The magic of books is that they allow each reader to create magic in their heads. Sometimes it's best left there.

Even at my impressionable age, I soon realized the actors were just people wearing costumes. That the magical town was just a quickly constructed set, and that half of the buildings were nothing more than false fronts, a single painted wall supported by struts creating giant empty right-angle triangles hidden from plain view.

Suddenly I could not see Mini Hollywood the same way, and I could not wait to get out of there. I wanted to keep the magic of my imagination intact. But it was too late, and not just for me in Tabernas.

Ever since then, I cannot visit a theme park or studio without immediately noticing the false fronts all around. Europa Park, Disney World, Universal Studios: No matter how artfully done, the entire experience is a set construction from beginning to end.

From the signage, the paint on the walls, the very flooring we walk upon, I see the craftsman's attempt to create worlds within worlds. It all seems so superficial because in my mind I know it has been built for effect. Sadly, the effect sought is less to create childlike wonder than to create the ideal conditions to separate weary parents from their money.

Why are these destinations still so popular, then, if we can easily recall at a moment's thought that they are nothing more than painted stages? Dear reader, it is because we want to be fooled.

We accept the false front as the reality because the reality behind the false front is just a hardscrabble desert or a reclaimed swamp. If life is hard and unforgiving, can we be blamed for wanting to believe in magic?

I suppose I can understand this, and could even forgive the impulse, if we did not take it so much further. We take at face value the whole of our lives.

We assume that what everyone else chases after must be valuable, so we chase after it too. We unquestioningly accept that buying things can bring us happiness, refusing to see the evidence before our eyes that though we are drowning in possessions we are no nearer to satisfaction.

We say "no good deed goes unpunished" as a cynical and self-serving way to justify focusing on our personal needs. I say, "No superficial thought goes unpunished," because in refusing to think for yourself, you resign yourself to accept the same fate as others.

How happy is your fellow person? How satisfied are they with their work, their pay, their politicians, their friends? How many suffer envy, greed, and misgivings, not to mention a hundred other maladies of the mind?

People say the Stoic philosophy is one of hardship and suffering because we try to see through the surface to the substance of things. When I compare the depth of mind of the average person with that of the philosopher, I must ask who is suffering the greater hardship.

What we gain from philosophy is deep peace of mind arising from confidence in our judgments and in our actions. The world is the same arid desert or reptile-filled swamp, but our steps are assured even though they are not always safe.

There is no greater achievement than to arrive at a point where you can look back on your life and say, "I would not change a thing."

Be well.

Chapter Twelve

On the AI Philosopher

Wisdom consists not just in making a correct decision, but in making it with an understanding of the reason why

You employ a most dangerous argument when you seek to use a lawyer's own words against them. In the present case, you have repeated back to me what I told you recently, namely that a wise person's reasoned judgment must come to the same conclusion when presented with the same facts.

You start with my conclusion, and you ask whether this means that a computer is wise. And taken a step further, will artificial intelligence become the ultimate embodiment of the wise philosopher, giving in to neither emotion nor temptation, providing consistently correct answers to all our problems?

Since it is my own words you employ, I cannot dismiss them lightly. Let me take you on a small journey before we arrive at our conclusion together.

Let us travel using one of the most impactful inventions of the Industrial Age, the combustion engine-powered car. The first modern automobile was invented in the 1880s by Karl Benz. If we could have an insight into horses' thoughts at that time, I wonder if they would have run something like this:

"Foolish humans. They have a perfectly reliable companion in us horses. We pull their loads, plow their fields, and take them to every corner of the earth. How much farther do they want to go, and how much faster do they want to get there? Can you ride two horses at once? Ten? And how will they feed them all? Mmmm, is that a carrot you're holding?"

Little did our faithful equine friends know how insatiable are our human appetites. Today mere passenger cars can sport more than a thousand HP, a veritable horde of horses to blanket the landscapes these supercars roar past.

Inside, their occupants are unseeing of anything they are speeding by beyond the tachometer and speedometer. My point is not to disparage the supercar or its owners, but rather to ask you this question: Is a horsepower equivalent to a horse?

"No one is suggesting that, and they never were" you say. "A horsepower is just a measure of power, the rate at which work is done."

All right. Is this a fairer comparison: Would you say a car is equivalent to a horse? Before you jump to answer, recall that it takes a combination of a car and a human to drive a car off a ferry landing and into a lake, something no horse would do.

You could say this is the fault of the human blindly following the GPS, but the car still ends up submerged. If a person sought to perform a similar stunt on their horse, the person is the one likely to end up spluttering wet.

"I know you said we were going on a journey" you say "but is it one that will take all day? Can we take a rest stop and stretch our legs?"

I am reminded of what young kids the world over say to their parents moments after getting in the car "Are we there yet?" And I will give the universal parents' response "Just a little bit further."

In place of our metaphorical rest stop and breath of fresh air let me just say that I am now preparing to compare the brain with the computer, our minds with the machine. I will even go so far as to give you the conclusion up front.

It is that today, and for the foreseeable future, I think, wisdom is a uniquely human attribute. Wisdom consists not just in making a correct decision, but in making it with an understanding of the reason why.

Humans make wise decisions out of more than short-sighted self-interest because they can anticipate consequences, both for themselves and others. A computer algorithm can make the same decision; indeed it cannot make any other, but there is no concern with consequences.

We talk of cold computer logic explicitly to distinguish it from humankind's reason, which is the result of overcoming our mess of constantly churning emotions. Though the resulting decision may be identical, the process by which we arrive at it couldn't be more different.

Some of the greatest advancements in artificial intelligence research came when we stopped trying to build algorithms to solve defined problems in their entirety and instead designed simpler systems patterned on human neural networks. This set the stage for deep learning and machine learning, where processing takes place in layers, each adding a piece of the puzzle and allowing higher levels of abstraction to emerge as a result.

In the case of both human infants and our fledgling machine systems, learning is the result of being confronted with data. Infants are amazing perception machines, taking in a flood of information from all their senses. This creates connections and associations among neurons in the brain, which are strengthened or weakened by further experiences.

The computer systems need to be force-fed their data like stubborn babies, and they need truly vast quantities of it to start drawing abstractions that a baby can do with ease.

It is when we observe how the two systems develop and learn from their steady diet of data that we come to the great distinction between humans and computers. Computers do not lack judgment. We humans build the rules in, or the rules for how rules will be learned, such that with a given input, the result will be the same.

What computers lack is perception. They do not sense the external world as we do, neither in quantity nor in quality. In fact, for any inputs to be made workable to the computer, they must be translated into the sterile binary code of zeros and ones. Humans do not lack perception. It is the judgment that we must learn through painful experience and repeated trial and error.

Because computers judge consistently but are limited in their perception, while humans have vast perceptions of situations that we judge inconsistently, we remain far apart.

And critically, when humans make judgments, it is the result of two things taken together: All of our past experiences and our anticipation of future results.

I have no doubt that we will steadily add to the situations in which computers outperform humans in tasks that appear to reflect perception, thinking, and judgment.

But until a computer takes the leap of making a decision not just because of past experience but because it desires a future outcome, I expect no wisdom to come from it.

Be well.

Chapter Thirteen

On Nature as a Guide

The philosopher is playing the happiness game that Nature also allows us to pursue by virtue of our reason

You have pointed out another inconsistency in the Stoic advice. Or at least you have raised a question about their consistency when you reminded me of a basic teaching I like to repeat.

"You have stated that we should strive in all things to live in accordance with Nature. This means being satisfied with the basics and not being tempted to chase after luxury. You also said that a major cause of our unhappiness is looking to see our relative position in the hierarchy, because no matter how many people we stand over, so long as there is one above us, we will be miserable."

So far so good, and I see no fault in the argument.

You continue "You also say, do you not, that hierarchy itself is a fundamental feature of Nature, and that every society and every group of animals will organize themselves according to hierarchies. In hierarchies, more possessions and power mean more status, which means a longer, more secure life with better mating opportunities. When the Stoics counsel us to become wise by foregoing the quest for more, are you not advising us to act against Nature?"

Although most who make such an argument are looking to justify their own insatiable desires, I know you are looking only to understand the truth of the matter. So, I will give your question the attention it deserves.

The first point I would make is that to say we should live in accordance with Nature is not to say that everything Nature offers is equally valuable.

I would rather recommend you live on the verdant slopes of a dormant volcano whose caldera has long since exploded and become still than on the lava-strewn plains of its active cousin. Both mountains are creations of Nature, but you may confidently choose the one that will provide a safe home for you and your family.

So too would I tell you to steer clear of the trackless desert and to take your guidance from the plants that Nature has deposited all around us. If a land is barren, why should we humans thrive there? The desert is just as much a part of Nature as the Alpine valley, but I can easily tell you which one we are better off dwelling in.

When we say live in accordance with Nature, this means first understanding your *own* nature. You can then take advantage

ON NATURE AS A GUIDE

of the resources Nature offers that provide the best match for your nature.

If you love the warmth and the feel of the sun on your face, better that you incline toward the equator. If you thrive in the cold, the Northern regions are a more suitable home for you.

The point is that the natural environments we find ourselves in differ. We can and should choose those environments that will best suit us. And this speaks only to physical needs.

The question you have raised goes a step further. You are asking how the hierarchies we so readily perceive are to be considered in accordance with Nature when they have such an impact on our minds and our state of mind.

Here we have come to the crux of the matter, dear reader. When we move from the physical to the mental, we arrive at the point where Nature ceases to be the primary driving force and humankind takes the wheel.

It is by our thinking, whether reasoned or not, that we make all that Nature offers better or worse.

- Nature provides the instinct for us to acquire more possessions, assert our dominance, and ascend the hierarchies we find ourselves in.

- Our thinking serves as a mechanism to accelerate or slow our progress, or to steer in another direction.

Do not forget, our minds are also the product of Nature. Thus, the application of our minds to the situations we find ourselves in is also acting according to Nature.

Does it seem like a conflict to you that one part of Nature drives us unthinkingly down certain paths while another part gives us the ability to look ahead and plot a course? I say no more a conflict than for every carnivore who eats today another creature has been killed.

And for that matter, who said Nature itself needed to be consistent in all things?

It is because humankind developed such keen reasoning that we are at risk of acting against Nature.

The animals around us do not amass possessions far beyond their potential use. When they have satiated their hunger, they stop eating. When they have slaked their thirst, they stop drinking.

It is humans who override the signals from Nature and drive themselves to new heights of avarice, gluttony, and greed. A need arises naturally and is satisfied naturally. A luxury is fabricated and requires an elaborate system to create and maintain.

So far, we are still talking about satisfying physical needs. Consider that as thinking creatures, we also have mental and emotional needs. I would place the desire to be happy high among them.

The philosopher's aim is to help achieve the conditions to live a good life. Here we see humankind's greatest danger to itself arises from itself.

Descartes did not go far enough with his famous statement "*cogito, ergo sum*." He needed to add a further word at the end: "I think, therefore I am unhappy." We are unhappy because we realize we could have more, and we see that someone else does have more.

I assert this is not thinking, but merely instinct run amok in our minds. Pesky Nature seeking to ensure humans are fruitful and multiply, and that only the strongest and fittest survive.

We are fruitful, dear reader, but it is now mainly in multiplying our problems and our worries. When the Stoics say to live in accordance with Nature by developing well-ordered reason to understand the true value of things, they mean that we should place the greatest value on our peace of mind.

The physical things we torment ourselves with are necessary for physical survival, and that is all. If we can relegate them to their proper place, we will see that our physical needs are relatively easy to satisfy.

Having satisfied our physical needs, we can then turn our attention to the regulation of our mental processes.

Our thoughts can make us either happy or unhappy. We are fools to become distracted by anything that experience shows leads to unhappiness.

Playing the status game is a consequence of the hierarchies Nature has established. The philosopher is playing the happiness game that Nature also allows us to pursue by virtue of our reason.

Be well.

Chapter Fourteen

On Instincts and Archetypes

We have the capacity to respond to our circumstances, and some responses will bring better results than others

You are not happy with my recent description of how humankind is to live in accordance with Nature. You think I have too quickly brushed past the physical needs of people to arrive at the emotional chaos that can only be tamed by well-ordered reason.

Thus, you ask me to remain for some moments more in the realm of the physical and address a separate question. How is it that nature provides animals with instincts to drive their survival and these instincts work to great effect, but in people those same instincts lead us to terrible outcomes?

Even though it is dissatisfaction that drives your question, dear reader, I take it up with the greatest satisfaction.

Teaching and learning are two sides of the same conversation, and in our talks, I find I learn as much as I try to teach. So, let's discuss this together and see if we may both come to a better understanding. As our prior assault on the fortress of knowledge was unavailing, let us try another avenue of attack.

For over two thousand years it was understood that physical traits acquired by an animal during its lifetime could be passed on to its offspring. In this way, creatures developed over time from simple things to ever more sophisticated beings.

The idea of inheritance of acquired characteristics came to be associated with the French zoologist Jean-Baptiste Lamarck in the early 19th century. His reputation was then tainted by the increasing number of scientists who failed to find solid evidence confirming the idea and came to associate Lamarck's name with the singular failure.

Later that century, Charles Darwin proposed the mechanism of natural selection as sufficient to explain the variations between and among species. The variation in starting conditions (creatures differ in their constitutions from birth) and in the environments they find themselves in means that some animals will be better suited for survival than others.

Darwin's mechanism of natural selection driving evolution has served us well as a conceptual framework for the last 150 years. How interesting, then, that there are recent developments that demonstrate once again it can be fruitful to approach conventional wisdom with a dose of caution, if not skepticism.

One development in particular offered a bridge between Lamarckism and Darwinism. Named after the American psychologist James Mark Baldwin, the Baldwin Effect deals with the fact that animals change their behavior in response to their environments.

The ones that learn the most successful new behaviors are more likely to reproduce, and hence *the propensity for learned behavior* is itself a natural characteristic that is then passed on via natural selection to the next generations.

I find this component of the modern synthesis of our understanding of evolution wonderful, dear reader, because it not only takes into account our mental processes but embraces them as a key driver of our progress through life.

We have the capacity to respond to our circumstances, and some responses will bring better results than others. From a survival perspective, the creatures most able to craft successful responses will be most likely to reproduce. We have physical instincts that drive us, but we also have mental characteristics that allow us to respond to our environments.

One of the earliest explorers into the mental realms that dwell within people and drive our actions was the Swiss psychologist Carl Jung. From his interaction with and observation of patients, Jung hypothesized that people possess what he called a collective unconscious, shared across time and culture.

He described archetypes as universal and recurring mental images or themes. It is a simplification to call archetypes instincts for mental processes, but the analogy suffices for our purposes.

Just as animals inherit instincts that drive their behavior, for example in avoiding certain dangers automatically, so humans inherit archetypes, a kind of innate knowledge of human behavior across history, that drive mental processes without our being consciously aware of it.

I have not forgotten your question, dear reader, and I hope you see that we are getting nearer to an answer. Thus far we have suggested that humans possess both physical instincts and mental instincts of a sort. I don't suppose you will contest that the mental processes of most humans are more advanced than those of most animals.

I think this helps explain why human instincts do not always operate to the same good effect that animal instincts do. It is because we can use our minds to *override* our positive instincts. Or as Canadian psychologist Jordan Peterson put it,

> Only man will inflict suffering for the sake of suffering. That is the best definition of evil I have been able to formulate.

We do not need to posit evil deeds to see that people inflict suffering on others. It is, moreover, undeniable that we also inflict suffering on ourselves. Sometimes the harm comes from being unaware of the consequences of our actions.

Just as often, I would say, people are willfully blind to the long-term consequences because they are stubbornly pursuing short-term gain. Perhaps it is a question of listening to the wrong instincts, or impulses if you will.

One of the boons of philosophy is slowing down and taking time to think. By evaluating actions and considering consequences we increase the chance that we will listen for and hear the voice of the collective unconscious, the instinctual archetype, calling out guidance.

If these things exist, they can be of great benefit to humankind because they allow us to put our base, physical instincts in their proper place. I won't say we can learn to override our negative instincts because I think every instinct evolved for a reason.

But when we use reason to consider our highest and best purpose, and then take action in accordance with that purpose, we are surely taking steps along the path to wisdom.

Hence, the very thing that leads people astray (using our mind to override positive instincts) also holds the key to our salvation.

Be well.

www.ingramcontent.com/pod-product-compliance
Lightning Source LLC
Chambersburg PA
CBHW060348050426
42449CB00011B/2877